PARTY GAMES FOR YOUNG CHILDREN

30p

Party

Drawings by
DORITIE KETTLEWELL

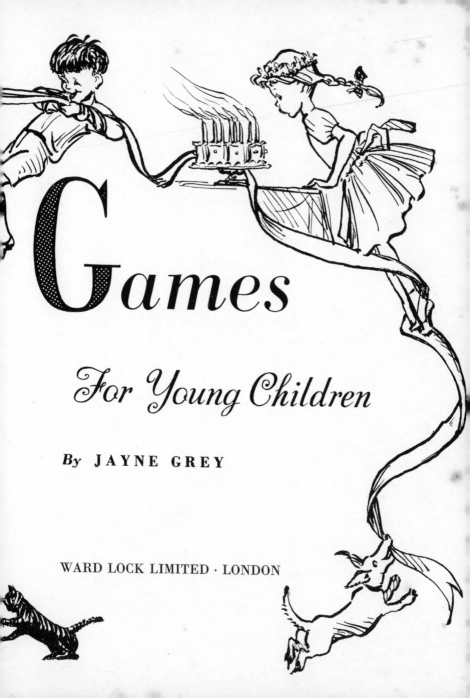

Games

For Young Children

By JAYNE GREY

WARD LOCK LIMITED · LONDON

© WARD LOCK & CO., LIMITED 1955

Second impression 1961

Paper-backed edition 1963

Reprinted 1967

Reprinted 1969

Reprinted 1971

Reprinted 1972

ISBN 0 7063 1040 3

We are grateful to Cadbury Brothers Ltd.,
for supplying the photograph used on the front cover

MADE IN ENGLAND

Printed in Great Britain by Fletcher & Son Ltd, Norwich

Contents

In compiling this book a great many works were consulted. Of particular interest and to which most reference was made are Alice B. Gomme's "Dictionary of British Folk-Lore", J. B. Pick's "Dictionary of Games", and Kate Stevens' "Party Games for All Occasions". I should also like to acknowledge the assistance of the librarians of the Folk-Lore Library and of the Westminster Reference Library.

Illustrations

Introduction

The wise general plans his campaign in advance, leaving as little to chance as possible. The wise parent plans her children's party with the same purpose and energy as the general. Awkward, unforeseen things will happen—not according to plan—but if the blue-print is sound, they will soon be coped with and forgotten.

Children LIKE to be organised. They may be unwilling to admit the fact, but fact it is, and it remains essentially true both in the classroom and at home. Plan your children's party, therefore, with care.

It does not come within the scope of this book to deal with refreshments, but a supply of home-made lemonade or orangeade, readily available, is greatly appreciated after a particularly energetic game, though it is advisable to keep a wary eye on the very young whose drinking capacity is limited by size, if not dictated by wisdom!

Patience, good humour, tact are standards any general would be proud to hoist and keep hoisted. Patience in directing games is so important that if you feel yourself on the edge of exploding just because that silly child refuses to stand in the right place, take a deep breath, scatter the

9

children, and leave the room. Come back, three minutes later, and start again!

Good humour and tact are closely allied to patience. Shy children will have to be persuaded to join the games; nervous children will show-off and upset the game without meaning to, while confident children will become truculent and difficult to manage if they feel they are not being made important enough.

Just as there are endless varieties of games to be played at any party, so there are endless varieties of children to be handled—or mis-handled—at any party. It is surprising how quickly the personality of little Miss Sarah Jones, aged 5, manifests itself during the first game. It is, therefore, a sound idea, if you do not already know something of the character of the small guests, to watch them quietly for a few minutes during the first game. Those with qualities of leadership will quickly show up, and you should file the information away in your mind for later on in the afternoon when you come to choose leaders for team games.

"What do we do NOW?" The question—if the party is going well—will be merely routine. A programme of games fixed on to the wall will give the information to those who can read. If the party is not going so well, the question is probably querulous, and means the children are not certain of themselves or of you. If you are wise, you will read from the programme: "Why, isn't that splendid, we are all going to play a game of 'Fox and Goose' next!"

The scope of this book is wide: outdoor as well as indoor games are suggested with simple instructions as to how to organise them. Few of the outdoor games need anything more complicated than an old pail or a ball, while nearly all the indoor games can be readily adapted, to any number, size or age group of children.

Older children sometimes quite surprisingly enjoy the "baby" singing games, while "babies" of course enjoy no greater compliment than being treated as "near-grown-ups"!

Many of the rhyming games have their roots in ancient soil going back hundreds of years; many of them too will be familiar to the children, although you will find they have all got their own ideas as to the method of playing, and even as to the words used in singing.

Never ask the children how to play. Make up your own mind first, and stick like a leech to your own set of rules. If necessary, begin: "Well, children, now this is how we play, just like the book says . . ." and if there is still mutiny in the ranks, produce the book! Children have a wholesome respect for the printed word.

And one last word. Some children are often slow to understand even the most simple instructions. Their friends will push and pull them into the right positions. Let them! Just watch patiently, until they are standing ready to listen—and then begin your explanation all over again—with a smile!

Singing Games

A singing game breaks down the initial barriers of shyness among small people. There is something so very friendly about being asked to stand in a ring hanging on to the hot and sticky hand of the boy next door whom you only see on the bus on Monday mornings.

Dusty Bluebells

When children are first introduced to this "running and singing game" they are thrilled by it, and the difficulty is sometimes to make them stop playing. It can be enjoyed by all ages and is best played in the garden or in a large room.

> *In and out the dusty bluebells,*
> *In and out the dusty bluebells*
> *Who is your master?*
> *Pittery Pattery on her shoulder*
> *Pittery Pattery on her shoulder.*
> *(Jeannie) is my master.*

One child is chosen, while the others form a ring holding hands and arching arms. As they begin singing, the leader skips in and out of the ring stopping finally behind one of her friends, whose shoulders she taps in time to the music. Jean then leaves the ring. She is now the leader, while the first child hangs on to her dress. They run in and out of the circle as the children begin the verse all over again, and as the game continues the train grows longer and longer and experiences considerable difficulty in wending in and out of the circle which has grown smaller and smaller. The last one to be chosen becomes the leader next time.

In and Out the Dusty Bluebell

Farmer Wants a Wife

This is such an old favourite that no apology is given for including it in this book, though the words will be familiar.

The farmer wants a wife,
The farmer wants a wife,
Hey Oh me daddy Oh,
The farmer wants a wife.

The wife wants a child,
The wife wants a child,
Hey Oh me daddy Oh,
The wife wants a child.

The child wants a nurse,
The child wants a nurse,
Hey Oh me daddy Oh,
The child wants a nurse.

The nurse wants a dog,
The nurse wants a dog,
Hey Oh me daddy Oh,
The nurse wants a dog.

The dog wants a bone,
The dog wants a bone,
Hey Oh me daddy Oh,
The dog wants a bone.

The dog wants a pat,
The dog wants a pat,
Hey Oh me daddy Oh,
The dog wants a pat.

HOW TO PLAY

The farmer is chosen and stands, glowing with pride, in the centre of the ring, which moves round him. He chooses a wife, who joins him in the ring, and then the wife chooses a baby, and so on. The climax comes when they all rush into the centre to pat the dog. Try and see to it that a fairly sturdy child is chosen as the dog. Sometimes the "pats" develop into "thuds" and the poor dog crumples under them.

Flower-pots

You first cross over,
And then cross back,
And step in the well as you cross the track,
And then there is something else you do,
Oh yes, you make a flower-pot too.

HOW TO PLAY

The children break up into groups of three to form a triangle, each with her left hand holding the right hand of the other; their hands being crossed in the centre. They skip and hop round to the music, any lively tune will do. Then they change hands, and skip in the opposite direction, Finally one of the three is chosen as the flower-pot and pushed into the middle (the well), leaving the other two to hop round her as best as they can. If the flower-pot is a big child, a lot of amusement is given through the efforts of the two small children to keep their hands tightly clasped as they dance round. The game continues until each of the three children has had a turn at being the flower-pot. This is a game for the very young.

Grand Old Duke of York

O the Grand Old Duke of York
He had ten thousand men,
He marched them up to the top of the hill,
And he marched them down again.
And when they were up, they were up,
And when they were down, they were down,
And when they were only half-way up—
They were neither up nor down.

Here is another excellent game with which to launch the party. The words and tune will probably be familiar to the grown-ups and some of the older children, but small children usually have to be introduced to this singing and clapping game.

HOW TO PLAY

Divide the children into two equal lines, giving them a little time to choose their own partners. The leaders join hands and skip (with a running side-step) down between the lines, while the words are sung, and the children clap their hands in time to the music. Down the line they go, and then up again. When they return to their first position the pair split up, one child marches down the back of her line, while her partner marches behind her own line; they meet at the bottom of the lines, and the new top couple are ready to skip down.

Hark the Robbers

Hark the robbers coming through,
   coming through, coming through,
Hark the robbers coming through
My fair lady.

They have stolen my watch and chain,
   watch and chain, watch and chain,
They have stolen my watch and chain,
My fair lady.

Off to prison they shall go, they shall
   go, they shall go,
Off to prison they shall go,
My fair lady.

Small boys enjoy this singing game almost as much as "Oats and Beans", perhaps because it tells a story.

HOW TO PLAY

Two boys join hands, holding them up as an arch for the other players to tramp through. The first two verses are sung first by one and then by the other of the two boys. At the finish of these, the child then going through the arch is stopped, and the third verse is sung with gusto. The prisoner is borne off and given a choice between a golden apple or a golden pear. Boys often prefer a more gruesome choice such as "Eaten by Lions", "Swallowed by Serpents". At any rate, whichever fate the victim elects to face, he is then sent to prison behind one or other of the leaders, and when all are captured, the inevitable tug-of-war follows.

London Bridge is Broken Down

And so it was! In the thirteenth century during the reign of Henry III! The song has been sung and piped all these hundreds of years—enough to make the Frenchman who built the bridge for King John turn restlessly in his grave! Here are the words:

> *London Bridge is broken down,*
> *Broken down, broken down.*
> *London Bridge is broken down,*
> *My Fair Lady.*

> *Build it up with silver and gold,*
> *Silver and gold, silver and gold.*
> *Build it up with silver and gold,*
> *My Fair Lady.*

HOW TO PLAY

Two children form an arch with raised arms, hands joined. The rest pass through, each holding on to the one in front, and hurrying to get past in safety before the bridge breaks. The last is caught by the descending arms of the first two children. Sometimes this is repeated until all the children have been caught and placed on the right or left, and the game ends with a tug-of-war. It is very similar to "Oranges and Lemons", but if the tug-of-war is not welcomed the captives could be asked to "pay a forfeit", *i.e.*, sing or dance or make an animal noise before the rest of the company. Make sure the shy guests are no longer "shy" before forfeit games are played, however.

Lubin Loo

Here we go lubin loo,
Here we go lubin li,
Here we go lubin loo
Upon a Christmas night.

Put all the right hands in.
Take all the right hands out.
Shake all the right hands together,
And turn yourselves about.

First verse repeat.

Put all the left hands in.
Take all the left hands out.
Shake all the left hands together,
And turn yourselves about.

First verse repeat.

Put all your right feet in.
Take all your right feet out.
Shake all the right feet together
And turn yourselves about.

First verse repeat.

Put all your left feet in.
Take all the left feet out.
Shake all the left feet together,
And turn yourselves about.

First verse repeat.

Lubin Loo

Put all your heads in.
Take all the heads out.
Shake all the heads together,
And turn yourselves about.

First verse repeat.

Put all the (Davids) in.
Take all the (Davids) out.
Shake all the (Davids) together,
And turn yourselves about.

First verse repeat.

Put All Your Left Feet In

And so on and so on, naming the different children in the ring. This game has a kind of hypnotic quality about it, for though it drags on endlessly, the players nearly always ask for more!

Muffin Man

Have you seen the Muffin Man,
The Muffin Man, the Muffin Man?
Have you seen the Muffin Man
Who lives in Drury Lane?

Yes, I've seen the Muffin Man,
The Muffin Man, the Muffin Man.
Yes, I've seen the Muffin Man
Who lives in Drury Lane.

HOW TO PLAY

A ring is formed by the players, who join hands. One child, who is blindfolded and holds a stick, stands in the centre. The children dance round, singing the verses. They then stand still and the child in the middle holds out the stick and touches someone in the ring. This player must take hold of the stick, and answer any question which the Muffin Man asks. He may ask: "Is coal blue?" etc., and she must reply in a disguised voice "Yes" or "No". Then the Muffin Man guesses who it is. He is allowed three tries, and if he guesses right, the child who was touched takes his place in the ring.

Mulberry Bush

Here we go round the mulberry bush,
The mulberry bush, the mulberry bush,
Here we go round the mulberry bush
On a cold and frosty morning.

This is the way we wash our hands,
Wash our hands, wash our hands,
This is the way we wash our hands
On a cold and frosty morning.

First verse repeat.

This is the way we wash our clothes,
Wash our clothes, wash our clothes,
This is the way we wash our clothes
On a cold and frosty morning.

First verse repeat.

This is the way we go to school,
Go to school, go to school,
This is the way we go to school,
On a cold and frosty morning.

HOW TO PLAY

This is a game for the very young. The children join hands and dance round in a ring to the first verse. Then they stop and suit their actions to the words of the second verse, and so it goes on. Obviously there are many things they can do, and these can be included in the verses, so that the game can go on for some time. On the last line of the first verse, they unclasp their hands and each turns rapidly round.

Nuts in May

Here we come gathering nuts in May,
Nuts in May, nuts in May,
Here we come gathering nuts in May,
On a cold and frosty morning.

Whom will you have for nuts in May,
Nuts in May, nuts in May?
Whom will you have for nuts in May,
On a cold and frosty morning?

We'll have . . . for nuts in May,
Nuts in May, nuts in May,
We'll have . . . for nuts in May,
On a cold and frosty morning.

Nuts in May

Who will you send to fetch her away,
To fetch her away, to fetch her away?
Who will you send to fetch her away,
On a cold and frosty morning?

We'll send . . . to fetch her away,
To fetch her away, to fetch her away,
We'll send . . . to fetch her away,
On a cold and frosty morning.

HOW TO PLAY

The children form in two lines of equal length, facing one another, with sufficient space between, to allow them to dance backwards and forwards, towards and away from each other, as each line sings the verses allotted to it. The first line sings the first and third and fifth verses, while the other lines sings the second and fourth. At the end of the fifth a handkerchief or scarf is laid on the ground and the two children mentioned engage in a tug-of-war.

Oats and Beans and Barley Grow

Both in England and America this is one of the most popular of the children's singing games, and is traditionally bound up with old harvesting customs. Here are the words:

> *Oats and beans and barley grow.*
> *Do you or I or anyone know*
> *How oats and beans and barley grow?*
> *First the farmer sows his seed,*
> *Then he stands and takes his ease,*
> *Stamps his foot and claps his hand,*
> *And turns about to view the land.*

HOW TO PLAY

The farmer stands in the middle of the ring. The game then merges into the usual choosing of a partner. The action of sowing the seed, etc., is imitated where the relevant words are spoken or sung. The boys in particular appreciate this game, deriving a hearty satisfaction from stamping the floor and viewing "their" land. There are many interesting variations in German, Swedish and Dutch of the words, and there are few countries in Europe where the children are not familiar with at least one form of "Oats and Beans"!

Oranges and Lemons

One of the most popular games among the 4 to 6-year-old age-group is the favourite "Oranges and Lemons". Children like to learn new words and rhymes, and there are always sure to be a few who do not know the words of this old song. You should make certain of them yourself before starting.

Oranges and Lemons

Oranges and lemons,
Sang the Bells of St. Clements.
You owe me five farthings,
Say the Bells of St. Martins.
When will you pay me?
Say the Bells of Old Bailey.
When I grow rich,
Say the Bells of Shoreditch.
When will that be?
Say the Bells of Stepney.
I'm sure I don't know
Says the great Bell of Bow.

Here comes a light to light you to bed.
Here comes a chopper to chop off your head.

The last two lines will appeal more to the blood-thirsty young members of the party.

HOW TO PLAY

The game is played in this manner. Two of the taller children stand facing each other, holding up their clasped hands. One is named "Orange" and the other "Lemon". The other players, grasping one another's frocks or trousers, run underneath the raised arms and round "Orange", and then under the arms again, and round "Lemon", while singing the verse. The last two lines are sung by "Orange" and "Lemon" in a slow menacing manner! At the word "head", they drop their arms over one of the children passing beneath their arch. She is then caught. They bear their prisoner out of reach of the hearing of the others and ask her in a piercing whisper whether she will be an

27

"Orange" or a "Lemon". The prisoner chooses her fruit. If she says "Orange" she then stands behind "Orange", her arms placed firmly round her friend's waist. The game continues until everyone engaged in it has ranged herself behind one of the leaders. When the two parties are ready, a tug-of-war takes place. It is wise to have a grown-up in authority at this stage. The winning side pulls the other side over a given mark. A good game for breaking down barriers, but some preliminary precautions are necessary. Small children's dresses may get torn if care is not taken during the tug-of-war match when excitement runs high.

"Which Shall It Be?"

Pop Goes the Weasel

Half a pound of tup'ny rice,
Half a pound of treacle,
Mix it up and make it nice.
Pop goes the weasel!

HOW TO PLAY

Another rhyme, which even the "babies" quickly pick up. The children stand in two rows facing each other. If there are boys at the party, the boys stand one side, the girls the other. They sing while moving backwards and forwards; retreat, advance—until the word "Pop", when the leader of each row chooses his partner from the line facing him; the others follow suit, then whirl each other round and round the room.

Ring a Ring of Roses

Ring a ring of roses
A pocketful of posies
Hush oh! Hush oh!
All fall down.

HOW TO PLAY

A ring is formed by the children joining hands. They all dance round singing the verse. At the words "Hush oh!" they sit suddenly down on the floor. This is one of the most ancient of our games and one which has been sung with enjoyment by little people for hundreds of years.

Tiny children are happy to play on without variation. Older children may demand that the last to "fall down" is out!

Thread the Needle

The children stand in two long rows, each holding the hands of their opposite number—the last two forming the arch. They sing:

> *Thread my grandmother's needle,*
> *Thread my grandmother's needle,*
> *Thread my grandmother's needle.*
> *Open your gates as wide as high*
> *And let King George and me go by,*
> *It is so dark I cannot see*
> *To thread my grandmother's needle.*

(Of course, they will want to change "King George" to "Queen Elizabeth!")

HOW TO PLAY

While the children sing, the others run under the raised arms, and when all have passed under, the first two hold up their hands, and so on, again and again, each pair in turn becoming the arch. It is interesting to note that children and their parents have been playing this game since 1738 at least and perhaps further back, and that in some English towns it is still played with enthusiasm on Shrove Tuesday.

Wally, Wally Wall-flower

Another singing game which is simple to play, but is quieter and much beloved by more thoughtful children. An excellent opportunity for the girls to display their "latest thing" in party dress as they parade round and round in a ring. The words are easily learned even by the very small.

Wally, Wally Wall-flower

Wally, wally wall-flower
Growing up so high—
We're all ladies
We shall all die
Excepting little . . .
She's the only one;
She can hop, she can skip
She can play the herald.
Fie! Fie, fie for shame
Turn your back to the wall again.

Wally, Wally Wall-flower Growing Up So High

HOW TO PLAY

The children form a ring by joining hands. They all dance slowly round singing the words. With the line "Excepting little . . ." the youngest child is named, and she turns round so that her face is turned to the outside of the ring and her back inside. She still clasps hands with those on either side of her, and dances round with them. The game continues until all the children are facing outwards.

31

Balloon Games

No party is complete without balloons and many and varied are the games which can be played with them.

The Balloon Race

Arrange three or four heaps of balloons (unblown of course) together with short pieces of wool, at one end of the room. At the word "Go" the children race towards the piles,

"I Had It First!"

select a balloon, and then blow. The winner is the child who returns to her place with her inflated balloon firmly tied.

Balloon Stick

This is a useful game to have in reserve if it is a small party. Choose two players and give them a balloon each and a short stick or piece of wood. In the centre of the room place a large basket or box. The idea is for the players to get their balloons into the box simply by using the sticks. They are disqualified if they use their hands or feet. The winner is the one who gets her balloon "home" first.

Balloon Waltz

Most children nowadays attend dancing classes and are familiar with the rudiments of ballroom dancing. If the party is a mixed one, each boy chooses a girl partner and waltzes round in time to the music. Round the ankle of each girl is tied a balloon, and when this bursts, the couple must leave the floor. Prizes are awarded to the pair whose balloon survives the general scrimmage.

All kinds of novelty balloons can be bought quite cheaply, and some very funny effects can be achieved by dressing up balloons which have got faces painted on to them.

Small children become distressed if their balloons burst, and the wise hostess will have a large supply in reserve to meet such emergencies.

A "Balloon Scatter", when a large number of balloons, of different shapes and colours, is let loose in the garden or indoors, is always popular even with the older children, and well worth the extra expenditure of a few shillings.

Indoor Games

From the outset, it is as well to be resigned to the fact that groups of children indoors will be noisy. A surprising amount of damage, too, can be done in a short time, and flower vases, ornaments, even pictures and photographs—so tempting to sticky fingers—should all be removed. But do get them out of the way *before* the children assemble.

Animal Noises Story

For very small children. This is a game which must have an adult or teenager in charge. The babies are grouped round the story-teller's feet. She gives each one the name of an animal. Then she starts telling the story, and it must be good! As she mentions "hens" all the hens in the audience cackle, and when she goes on to "dogs" all the dogs bark. The under-fours love this type of entertainment, but much of the fun depends on the skill of the story-teller.

Blindman's Buff

Children are apt to demand this game in much the same spirit as their grandfathers and grandmothers did before them. A responsible person should always hold watching brief over all games that involve blindfolding, because accidents will and do happen. A guard must be placed across the fire when children are playing such games indoors, and indeed this rule should in any case be rigidly observed when children are playing games in any room where there is a fire.

A steady, sensible child should be chosen as the Blindman. He shuffles after the children, and when he catches one, the victim must giggle or make the noise of an animal to help him to guess who it is. If he guesses correctly, the two change places.

Blind Postman

This is a quieter and less dangerous version of "Blindman's Buff". Children from 8 to 10 years old enjoy it without becoming over-excited. Each player takes the name of a town. A circle is then formed, and one child, the postman, stands blindfold in the centre and calls two town names. As the children all quietly change their seats, Postie gropes his way to what he hopes is an empty chair, and if he is lucky ends his career.

Bobbing Apples

Older children enjoy "Bobbing Apples" and the babies enjoy watching. Drop a number of rosy-red apples into a tub of water. (Newspaper or an old bath mat will protect the carpet.) The children then take it in turns to kneel on a chair, an ordinary kitchen chair, not too high, is best. They rest their arms on the back, head over the tub, with a fork between their teeth. The idea is to drop the fork on to an apple so as to pierce it. It is much less simple than it sounds, but the children never seem to get tired of trying.

Bunny Hop

Before starting this game, encourage the children to practise "bunny hops". They will enjoy it! All the children are "bunnies" except three of the bigger ones. These are the "ferrets". On the word "Go!" the bunnies leave their burrows and hop about freely, while the ferrets remain quietly in their corners. At the word "Now!", the ferrets go into action, on all fours, and try to catch as many bunnies as possible before they reach the safety of their burrows.

Cat and Mouse

The very title brings a glint into the children's eyes. The room should be cleared of obstacles as far as possible. The little ones enjoy this game because no child can resist the excitement of a chase, but it is a game which should be carefully supervised by a grown-up.

The children, any number, form a ring in the centre of the floor. Their arms are extended, and hands clasped. The "mouse" is chosen and goes outside the circle. She tiptoes round quietly for a second or two, then gently pulls the frock of one of the children in the ring. The Cat! The cat now chases the mouse in and out of the ring until she catches her. Then the mouse takes the place which the cat formerly occupied, and cat becomes mouse and the game starts all over again.

This game is known also as "Drop the Handkerchief", and is less exciting and therefore perhaps more suited to tiny children, under this title. A child is chosen; she is given a handkerchief, and moves quietly in and out of the ring, until she makes up her mind; then she drops the handkerchief (usually behind her best friend). The chase then follows. When she is caught, she takes her best friend's place in the ring, and the best friend carries on with the handkerchief.

Cinderella and Prince Charming

This is a game for a fairly large party, and is popular among children of the Middle East. A large ring is formed. Prince Charming is chosen and blindfolded. Cinderella is then chosen silently, and unknown to the Prince. The two children are then placed inside the ring, as far from each other as possible. They then call each other by name, but they must not have any other conversation. When Prince Charming has caught Cinderella he has to guess who she is. If he guesses wrongly another Cinderella is chosen and he has to try again. If he guesses correctly, two new children are chosen and the game starts again.

Do This, Do That

A useful game to ensure some quiet moments after a romping session and one which can be played by the young and not-so-young. One child calls out commands beginning "Do this" or "Do that". If he says "Do this", the players do it; if he says "Do that", they don't. Anyone who performs an action on the command "Do that", drops out of the game, and the last player left in wins.

This game is sometimes known as "Sammy Says Thumbs Up". The principle is exactly the same. The children sit round Sammy, who says the words, and they put up their thumbs. If he is cunning, he will go on repeating "Sammy says thumbs up" for some moments, then suddenly remark "Thumbs up". The players who raise their thumbs on this command are out.

Dove Flutter

A very charming game played by children in Eastern lands; One of the bigger girls takes hold of the hands of two of the smaller children, one of whom represents a dove and the other a hawk. The hawk stands behind her, and the dove in front. She throws the dove away with a very pretty gesture of her hands, and as the child runs it waves its arms as though they are wings. She then throws the hawk in the same way and it follows the dove. After a little time, she claps her hands (the Chinese always do this to recall their pet birds) and the dove if not caught returns to the cage. Little children love this game, which is so pretty to watch, especially if it is played in the garden—with trees and shrubs to hide behind.

Down in the Jungle

Small children, especially small boys, adore this game because it is noisy! The more children taking part the better, and any number from twelve upwards is satisfactory. If twelve are playing, three children elect to be lions, two to be elephants, four to be tigers, and so on. Lions, elephants and tigers, etc., then jumble themselves up behind two base lines at opposite ends of the room. The hunter stands in the middle and calls out an animal group, who then advance, trumpeting or roaring as the case may be, from opposite base lines. The hunter, approached from both directions, tries to grab one of the animals, and any beast caught helps the hunter in the next safari!

Fox and Geese

Another game which provides fun in a large room or the garden. Mother Goose is at the head of a long file of her "babies" who clasp each other firmly round the waist. Flapping her wings and sticking her neck out, Mother Goose leads her little ones all over the room in an effort to evade Mr. Fox, who tries to pounce on the last baby in the line. This game is most suitable for the very young, who play it with great gusto and enjoyment.

Giant's Treasure Store

This is also a game for the very young, and for any number of players from six to twenty. The giant, one of the bigger children, lies on the floor. Beside him is his treasure; a collection of reels, curtain rings, beads, bangles, etc. He is fast asleep, and snores realistically. The other small children try to advance, but if he looks at them they must "freeze". When they feel safe again they move forward. When one of the treasures is seized, the robber starts back towards her den, and the giant rushes after her. If he succeeds in catching her, she drops out of the game. Anyone seen moving also drops out.

Grandmother's Footsteps

This is a game for the very young. Grandmother stands at one end of the room, her back towards the players who are lined up at the other end of the room. Whenever she whirls round they must stop advancing. If she spies any of them moving, she sends them back to the starting line again. The first to touch Grandmother's shawl claims the honour of being the next Grandmother. In Scotland this game is known as "Charlie Come Over the Water", and dates back to the days of Prince Charles who sought refuge, at one time, in France.

Hedgehogs

A game for the 5 to 6-year-olds. If there are only six or seven at the party, this is a good game because it introduces a novelty note. Each child is presented with a fairly large and, if possible, oblong-shaped potato, a saucer of pins and a pair of small scissors. At the word "Go", she must pick up the pin with the scissors and stick it into the potato. A responsible and alert grown-up slowly counts up to twenty. The winner is the one who has given the hedgehog the greatest number of spines. A few sticks of plasticine will allow the children to make the head and legs, and add considerably to their pleasure in the game.

A word on plasticine. There are now some very good makes on the market, and small children in the 4 to 6 age-group are always pleased to play with this. They must, of course, be watched, otherwise the raspberry colour may disappear inside Mary Jane. Interest and enthusiasm are easily aroused. A prize could be awarded for the best monkey, or the best house, or the best Noah's Ark. But do remember to put down a sheet of newspaper on the table before allowing the children to start.

Honey-pots

Honey-pots, honey-pots, all in a row,
Twenty-five shillings wherever you go.
Who'll buy my honey-pots?

A Good Little Honey-pot

This is just one of several rhymes for the game of "Honey-pots", in which one child clasps his hands under his knees while two others lift him by the armpits and swing him to and fro. This is an ideal game for the mixed party. If his hands remain clasped throughout the verse he is a good honey-pot, but if he fails to keep his hands clasped, he is a broken honey-pot and gets swept away. Small children love this game, and the older, stronger children enjoy swinging the little ones.

How Many Teeth, Mr. Bear?

Mr. Bear sits gloomily inside a circle. The others advance and pertly ask him: "How many teeth, Mr. Bear?" If the bear growls "Two", or any other number, they are quite safe; but if he suddenly mumbles "Twenty—very sharp", they must fly for home for the bear is after them. All he tags drop out of the game. For the very young!

Hunt the Slipper

All the players, but one, sit on the floor in a circle with their legs crossed (Turkish fashion). These are the cobblers, and under the eagle eye of their master, they must pretend to work very hard at making or mending shoes. Presently a customer appears carrying a slipper. She goes up to the Master Cobbler and says:

> *Cobbler, cobbler, mend my shoe,*
> *Get it done by half-past two.*

Master Cobbler accepts the shoe, and the customer goes away, to return a few seconds later to ask if the shoe is ready. The Cobbler replies: "No, not quite. Call again in an hour's time," or makes some other excuse. When she calls again, she is told that the shoe has been sent home. The customer vows she will make a search. The Cobblers in the ring all place their hands under their knees, and pass the slipper secretly from one to another in such a way as to prevent the owner of the shoe getting it for some time. The Cobbler from whom she at last recovers her shoe becomes the next customer.

Children love "Pretend Games", and in this Cobbler Game there is scope for a certain amount of miming which they enjoy. It is suitable for very young people.

I Packed My Bag

The children sit in a circle on the floor or on chairs in rows. The first begins: "I packed my bag for London, and in it I put . . ." she then adds whatever article she wishes, say a "brush". The next child starts off: "I packed my bag for London and in it I put a brush and a golliwog . . ." And so on. Some children are extraordinarily good at remembering, and the contents of one case sometimes number more than thirty articles before the game comes to an end. A very useful stand-by when little hands are hot and sticky, and little legs are tired with rushing about.

I Wrote a Letter

> *I wrote a letter to my love,*
> *And on the way I dropped it.*
> *I dropped it, I dropped it*
> *And on the way I dropped it.*

One child is chosen, and given a letter. The other children are seated in a circle. The child with the letter runs round the outside of the ring, repeating the words over and over again and at one point drops the letter behind one of the players, who must pick it up and chase the dropper. The letter-dropper tries to reach the vacant place first, and if she succeeds, the child without a place in the ring becomes the letter-dropper. A second verse adds zest to the game: Here it is!

> *I wrote a letter to my love*
> *And on the way I dropped it.*
> *Some of you have picked it up*
> *And got it in your pocket, pocket, pocket.*

Children of all ages enjoy this game.

Johnny Rover

> *I warn ye ance, I warn ye twice;*
> *I warn ye three times over;*
> *I warn ye a't'be witty and wise*
> *An' flee frae Johnny Rover.*

One player is chosen to be Johnny Rover. When the rhyme is finished the other players run off pursued by Johnny Rover. The first to be caught becomes Rover in turn. This is a good game which small boys enjoy, especially small Scottish boys, providing there is ample space.

Jumble Sale

Some preparation is needed for this game, which is best played in a fairly large room. Arrange a number of articles, the odder the assortment the better, at the far end of the room. There should be two or three *fewer* articles than players. The children are then lined up some distance away, and at the word "Go" race towards the "Jumble Sale". Those who are not quick enough to grab any of the articles fall out, and the game continues. Remember to remove one or two objects each time.

In the same class as "Jumble Sale" is "Quick Change". A number of articles of clothing are arranged on a long table or on chairs at one end of the room or garden. Each child must dress himself in a hat, sock and shoe provided, then race back to the starting line. First back is the winner. After a game of this nature, even the shyest child is likely to "open out". If the party is a mixed one, the little boys may be given ties instead of hats, and the girls ribbons instead of socks. There are many ways of overcoming "clothing shortages".

Jumping the River

This is a game which can be played in a large room with lots of space, or better still in the garden. A river is made, using string or brightly coloured wool. Narrow at the source, it gradually grows wider and wider as it flows on. The children line up in an orderly manner, one behind the other, at the narrowest point, and each in turn tries to jump across. If they clear the river they must do a standing-jump back. If they fall in, then their feet are now wet and they must drop out of the game to change their socks. The successful jumpers move higher and higher up river, until only one, the winner, is left with dry feet.

Kipper Race

If the number of children is fairly small, the "Kipper Race" is the kind of novelty game which can be played in a fairly large room or outside in the garden providing there is not too much wind! The outlay is negligible. A large sheet of tissue-paper will provide the kippers, which should be cut out as realistically as possible. At one end of the room space out a number of plates or saucers. The children are then lined up at the other end. Each one is given a fish and a magazine or folded newspaper with which to flip the kipper towards his plate. Anyone touching the kipper with his magazine is disqualified. The first child to "land" his fish wins the game.

Mary's Sunbonnet

This is one of the quieter but very funny team games which can be played indoors. Two small baby bonnets are provided. The leader of each team must put one on, tie the strings in a bow under his chin (no cheating allowed). Next child unties bow, places bonnet on head, and does it up neatly. Mary's bonnet thus travels down the line!

Minister's Cat

Another quiet, sitting game for children and grown-ups. The idea is to describe the minister's cat by using up all the letters in the alphabet, one by one. For instance, Bill starts off: "The minister's cat is an *angry* cat", and Jean, next to him, continues with: "The minister's cat is an *ancient* cat"; and so on until the letter "a" is exhausted.

46

Murder in the Dark

The 10-year-olds will exclaim enthusiastically when this game is proposed, but it is not a game for nervous, excitable children. As it is very much in demand these days, however, a clear picture of the "set-up" is extremely useful. Folded slips of paper are first prepared by the Master of Ceremonies; on one slip is marked a cross, on another a circle. The child who draws the cross is the murderer and gives no sign. If the children are playing this game for the first time this will have to be very clearly emphasised before the proceedings. The child who draws the circle is detective and loudly proclaims the fact to all and sundry.

All taking part scatter throughout the house, and the lights are turned off. Some reservation might be made here, *i.e.*, only

"Mary's Sunbonnet Might Look Well on Me!"

47

three rooms need be used, but this will depend very much on the discretion of the organiser. The murderer then performs his dark and dirty deed preferably in a lonely place, crying loudly "You're dead!" and the poor victim screams and the lights are turned on.

The detective studies the corpse as soon as the lights go on, keeping a wary eye open for signs of movement among the onlookers. One of the rules of the game is that each person must give a truthful reply when he asks them a question. The murderer, however, may tell as many "fairy stories" as he can think up, until he is asked point-blank: "Did you do it?" If the cap fits, he must then say: "Yes, I did it!" Young players are generally allowed three guesses, and the detective if he fails in his detecting after the third attempt pays a forfeit to the murderer, who now smugly confesses his guilt. The same folded slips of paper are replaced in the hat and the game starts again. If small children look nervous, send them with a big "sister".

Discerning parents will realise the drawbacks of playing this type of game with small children, but to be forewarned is to be forearmed, and if they know the rules and the snags, they will be able to take a firm line when the game is proposed.

NOTE ON MUSICAL GAMES

Music is a useful background to any kind of game, and children never seem to mind however "tinny" the old gramophone sounds. But there are a few games for which music is essential, and these are detailed in the following pages. It is advisable to have a teenager in charge of the wireless or gramophone. A piano is a useful asset to the party, and the pianist need not worry if her repertoire is somewhat limited.

Musical Chairs

Any number up to about twenty. There should be one less number of chairs than children, and these are placed in a circle. A gramophone, piano or wireless (providing there is an obliging programme of light music) is essential. Players walk or hop or dance round the chairs in time to the music. When it stops suddenly, the child failing to secure a chair is out. Another chair is then removed, and the game proceeds. The last left in wins the game.

If chairs are limited in supply, "Musical Bumps" is enjoyed just as much by the small people. In this case, the child who is the slowest in falling to the ground when the music stops is out, but it is advisable to have a responsible person in charge so that there are no squabbles over who is out!

Musical Hotch-potch

A number of articles, beads, toys, nuts, or any other small object, is placed in the centre of the room. The game is more amusing if the articles in themselves are funny! The children hop around the pile in time to the music. When it stops, they each dive for an article. If ten children take part, there should be, of course, nine articles. The child who fails to secure an object is out, and so is one of the oddities! A certain zest is given to the game if the winner is allowed to keep the object she finally retrieves!

Musical Magic Carpet

Another dancing game which children enjoy because it has a grown-up flavour is "Magic Carpet". The children all dance or jog round in pairs to a lively tune. They are told that somewhere on the "Magic Carpet" is a "Magic Patch", which has been previously decided upon by the hostess. When the music stops the pair standing on the "Magic Patch", or nearest to it, are awarded small prizes.

Musical Parcel

This is a good game to follow the energetic "Musical Bumps". A small prize is wrapped up into an inviting-looking parcel. The children stand or sit in a circle. When the music stops, the child holding the parcel drops out. Gradually, the players are eliminated, one by one, until the last man in is the only one left in the ring, and he is proclaimed the prize-winner.

Musical Statues

Another game which lends itself to a party where there are juniors and seniors present. The children each take a partner and dance round the room in time to the music. If the person in charge of the gramophone is cunning enough, they will be caught out when the music suddenly stops, but she should remember that the children will watch her movements with eagle eyes. When the music stops they must become statues. If they are seen moving, they must sit down and watch the others; they can help with the decisions at the end of each round. Prize for the winning couple.

Noah's Ark

For the very young! Two small children are chosen as Mr. and Mrs. Noah, and stand at the door of the Ark. The rest of the children are then paired off. One line is the "Mr." animals and the other line the "Mrs." animals. Each couple in turn go to the Ark, "Mr." acting what he is, and "Mrs."

"Assorted Sizes, but we Still Keep in Step!"

(who does not know) copying him as closely as possible. Mr. Noah then says: "Who comes for a home in the Ark?" Mrs. Animal has to answer. If she is right they enter, if wrong they are drowned in the flood!

Nose in the Matchbox

A game for older children, but one which gives a good deal of amusement. The teams are again in two lines facing each other. The leader of each side is given an empty matchbox cover which he fixes on to his nose. The idea is to pass the matchbox from nose to nose right down the team. No hands are allowed, and any member of the team who touches the box with his hands or drops it altogether disqualifies his side. Boys especially like this game, and it is a useful one to produce when the hostess wants a few quiet moments in the kitchen.

O'Grady

Before starting the game, ask the children to have some forfeits ready. These may be hats out of their crackers, or sweets, or trinkets. The leader is called O'Grady, and he explains that whatever he asks must be done, or he will collect a forfeit. Then he starts off: "O'Grady says . . .", but if he should suddenly begin his order without first saying "O'Grady says", the children must *not* obey him. If they do, they are "caught out" and must pay a forfeit. Some very amusing moments can be had depending on O'Grady's ingenuity. A game for all ages.

Popping the Bag

For the more sophisticated 10-year-olds this team game provides a good deal of amusement. Divide the number into two teams. Arrange two rows of chairs facing each other with a paper bag on each. The leaders of the teams start the game by leaving their chairs, each scampering down his row, back to his place, when he must blow up the paper bag and then burst it. The next member of the team may not leave his chair until he hears the "pop". And so it goes on. Whichever side "pops" all the bags first, wins.

"Have I Puffed Out the Candle Yet?"

Puff in the Dark

What child fails to enjoy blowing out the candle! This game, however, should be carefully supervised. A lighted candle is placed on a table; it should stand in a solid receptacle so that any danger of the candle being knocked over is avoided. A child is then blindfolded and gently turned round three times. She is then told to blow out the candle and is allowed three puffs. The successful "puffer" is the winner, and a small prize such as a bar of chocolate or a little packet of sweets will greatly add to the pleasure of the game.

Puss in the Corner

Another "pussy" game for the energetic 4-year-olds. This game is better played with a few rather than with many, and requires a cleared space in the centre of the room, with nothing breakable within a hundred miles! Puss is chosen, and stands in the middle of the room chanting "Poor Puss wants a corner! Poor Puss wants a corner!" The others, who are standing in their corners or dens, must now move, and if Puss is smart she will find herself a vacant den all right, and the child left homeless then becomes Puss.

In Scotland this game is called "Moosie in the Corner"— an endearing title to any child from Scotland finding herself at an "English" party. If the game is played in a room, as many chairs are placed as there are players, *less* one. Each takes a seat and one—the Moosie—is left standing. On the word "change", which Moosie calls, each child jumps from the seat and makes for another. It is then Moosie's business to find herself a "corner", and the child left without a chair becomes the next Moosie.

Puzzle Find the Ring

Grown-ups as well as children enjoy this game. Arrange the group into a circle with Peter in the middle of it. Tell him he has to try and see who has the ring when the music stops. The ring, which is on a long strand of stout wool knotted at the ends, passes secretly from hand to hand as the children allow the wool to slip quickly through their fingers. They

Puss Has Found a Corner at Last

must try to keep the ring itself invisible. Then the music stops. Peter points to the child he suspects is holding the ring, and if he is right he joins the circle and the child "caught out" takes his place in the middle. Very small children should be allowed to have some practice shots first as they may find the wool hard to manage, but the advantages of playing such a game are twofold. No prize is called for, and young and old may take part in it without loss of dignity!

Ruby Ring

My Lady's lost her ruby ring
I fix on you to find it!

One of the children is chosen as the servant and is given a ring. The other children then stand in a ring or in a line with their arms straight down in front of them, their hands forming a cup, which is partly hidden by their knees. The servant keeps the ring hidden in the palm of her hands which are pressed close together. As she walks slowly round the ring, she chants the above words, while quietly dropping the ring into somebody's palm. She touches everybody's

My Lady's Lost Her Ruby Ring

56

hands so that the deception is more complete. Then she returns to the first child and repeats the words in an accusing tone. This child now tries to guess who has the ring. The servant then moves on to the next child, and so on, until she has been right round the ring. Those who guess right escape, but the others who have guessed wrongly must pay a forfeit.

Shopping

Here is a game which delights the small children, and is original but very simple to play. A number of coloured discs (halfpennies if there is money to spare) are hidden round the room. A small stall with a few good things on it is prepared in the centre of the room and one of the older children is put in charge. Little packets of coloured sweets, a few nuts, an apple, or perhaps some tiny toys from crackers, are displayed. As soon as one of the children finds a piece of "money" she rushes to the shop and buys herself whatever she fancies. When all the "money" is handed over, a new shopkeeper is chosen, and the game starts again.

Spinning the Platter

This is a good game to start off with if the guests are in the 8 to 10 age-group. One of them stands in the centre of the ring, holding a large meat plate. She bends down, and as she spins the plate, calls out the name of one of the children, who must dash forward and catch the plate before it drops. Then the new spinner repeats the process. Sometimes it is better to have a grown-up as the first spinner, but even the smaller children quickly manage to "birl" the plate, and the state of expectation they get into while waiting to hear their names chases away all that initial shyness which sometimes afflicts children at the beginning of a party.

Statues

A peaceful game and sometimes very pretty to watch! Any age-group enjoys it. The children line up, one is chosen as Mr. Sculptor. He goes up to number one in the line, grasps her firmly by the hand and whirls her out into the room. When he releases her hand, she must strike a pose. With older children it can be arranged beforehand what sort of characters they are going to try and become, *i.e.*, historical, comic, tragic, etc. When all the children have been turned into "statues", Mr. Sculptor tries to guess what each one is meant to be. Any child who moves after he has been "sculped" falls out of the game.

Statues Advance!

This is similar in a way to "Statues" and is enjoyed by active children. Mr. Sculptor turns his face to the wall and slowly counts up to twenty or ten or whichever number he pleases. The others are lined up at the other end of the room. The idea is to advance secretly on Mr. Sculptor without letting him see them move. When he whirls round, they must strike an attitude and keep it up as long as the Sculptor looks at them. If they move even a little finger they are out. When he turns once again to face the wall, they drop their pose and scamper forward. The first to touch his sleeve is the winner, and becomes Mr. Sculptor next time. With older children, the Sculptor may dictate the pose by ordering— "Funny", "Sad", etc., as he faces the wall.

"Guess What I'm Meant to Be!"

Thimble Hunt

One child hides an article, it need not be a thimble, while the other children, the seekers, adjourn outside the room. When they return, the hider is allowed to help them by saying "hot", or "very hot", "scorching", "burning", etc., if they are very close to the hidden article; or "cold", "very cold", "freezing", if they are looking in quite the wrong direction.

Sometimes all the party assist in hiding the thimble, while only one child is the seeker. To guide the seeker in her search, they sing nursery rhymes or popular tune hits:

loudly if the child is "warm", very softly if she is "cold". This is a pleasant variation on the hum-drum "Hide-and-Seek", and can safely be played without much supervision.

Tiggly-Wiggly Snake

This is a romping game requiring plenty of space. One of the bigger children is chosen as the snake and given a house. At the word "Go" he leaves home to try and catch something for his supper. When he catches his first victim, she must hold his hand, and the two then continue to chase and catch. Each victim caught takes the hand of the last victim, so that eventually the snake heads quite a long line. If the children in the snake let go their hands, the snake breaks up, and its members run home. The snake then reassembles and starts out again to catch the others. The last child to be caught wins the game.

Tiggy-tiggy

Tiggy-tiggy touchwood, my black hen,
She lays eggs for gentlemen.
Sometimes eight and sometimes ten
  (nine and so on),
Tiggy-tiggy-touchwood, my black hen.

The children may not be familiar with this rhyme, but they will soon pick it up, and when they do, want to go on chanting it forever! Players may not be captured so long as they are touching "wood". Tiggy, one of the bigger children, stands some distance away. The others advance and the fun is in the daring sorties they make in order to tempt Tiggy to run after them. As he clutches them, the children change the number in the verse.

Tom Cat and Miss Mouse

"What o'clock is it?"
"Just struck nine."
"Is the Mouse at home?"
"He's about to dine."

"You Can't Catch Me! Or Can You?"

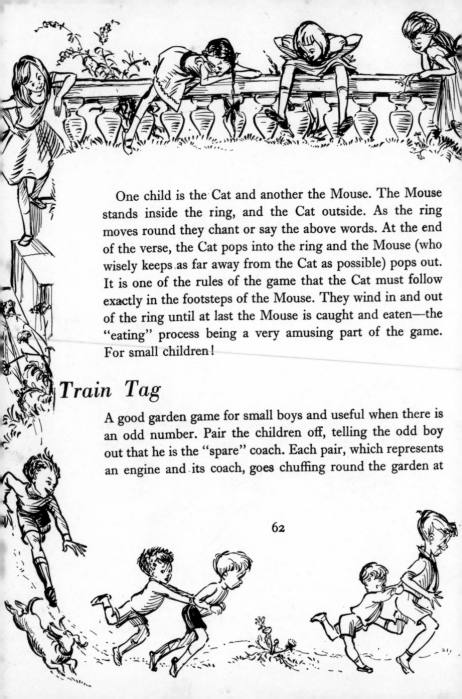

One child is the Cat and another the Mouse. The Mouse stands inside the ring, and the Cat outside. As the ring moves round they chant or say the above words. At the end of the verse, the Cat pops into the ring and the Mouse (who wisely keeps as far away from the Cat as possible) pops out. It is one of the rules of the game that the Cat must follow exactly in the footsteps of the Mouse. They wind in and out of the ring until at last the Mouse is caught and eaten—the "eating" process being a very amusing part of the game. For small children!

Train Tag

A good garden game for small boys and useful when there is an odd number. Pair the children off, telling the odd boy out that he is the "spare" coach. Each pair, which represents an engine and its coach, goes chuffing round the garden at

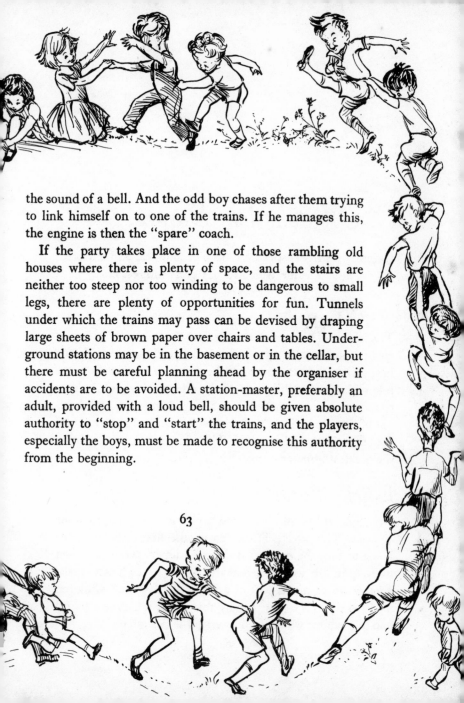

the sound of a bell. And the odd boy chases after them trying to link himself on to one of the trains. If he manages this, the engine is then the "spare" coach.

If the party takes place in one of those rambling old houses where there is plenty of space, and the stairs are neither too steep nor too winding to be dangerous to small legs, there are plenty of opportunities for fun. Tunnels under which the trains may pass can be devised by draping large sheets of brown paper over chairs and tables. Underground stations may be in the basement or in the cellar, but there must be careful planning ahead by the organiser if accidents are to be avoided. A station-master, preferably an adult, provided with a loud bell, should be given absolute authority to "stop" and "start" the trains, and the players, especially the boys, must be made to recognise this authority from the beginning.

Matchstick Games

Games with matchsticks are both economical and amusing. A very simple game which rouses great interest is:

Steal-a-stick

The children sit round a table. In the centre is a bag of spent matches. One of the children tips the contents into a heap. Each child in turn must then remove a match from the pile without disturbing any of the others. If any of the surrounding matches move while she is doing this, she drops out of the game. This is a game which holds the attention of the children to the bitter end. The winner is the one who has the greatest number of matches in front of her.

Matchstick Words

One child starts off by placing a match in any position she chooses. The next child builds on the first stick, the idea being to turn the original stick into a letter. Words are then built up in this way. When anybody fails to see how to make a letter which forms part of a word, she falls out. Children in the 8 to 10 age-group enjoy this game, which is a useful one to produce when a quiet session is desirable.

Mr. Walking-match

For the small party, this is an original and amusing pastime requiring very little preparation. Each child is given a knife—an ordinary table or kitchen knife—a match, and a little cut-out figure of a man or boy; scraps or diminutive figures cut from cartoons would do very well. They are then told to bend the match in half, making a prong, and on top of the prong to fix the picture of the man. (It would be more satisfactory if a grown-up demonstrated the idea first.) They must then place the inside of the prong upon the edge of the blade of the knife, and hold the latter parallel with the table, so that both ends of the match just touch the surface. The match will then "walk" from one end of the knife to the other, without any effort on the part of the knife-holder. When the children understand what it is all about and have had some practice "tries", arrange a race. The child whose Mr. Match reaches the end of the knife first, wins, and a small prize will put the finishing touch to an unusual game which the players will long remember.

At Least One Mr. Match is Ready for the Race

Acting Games

Children enter into any Pretence Game with such enthusiasm that it is disappointing when Acting Games are left out of the party. If it is practicable a pile of old clothes, such as men's hats, scarves, even a cast-off summer dress or two, can greatly add to the enjoyment of the actors and audience. In all such games, the patient, kindly advice of a grown-up is necessary if endless wrangling over who-is-going-to-play-what is to be avoided. One group of children consist of the audience, while the others retire outside the room, preferably with someone older in charge. If they are going to act historical characters, etc., they decide on incidents, select a suitable one, allocate parts to each other, and then return to the room. The audience are allowed six guesses as to what it is all about.

Dumb Charade

Among the older children, the game of "Charades" is a firm favourite. Divide the players into two equal lots. One group is the audience and the other group the actors, and they must go outside the room and choose their word. If the children are under 9 a nursery rhyme is best, or the title

"Does Everybody Know How to Act?"

of a pantomime. When the actors have decided on their rhyme, they then come in and act it before the audience. If the audience guess what the rhyme or pantomime is, then they adjourn outside, and the actors become the audience. This is a good game to suggest half-way through the party, when the children are fairly tired but "won't lie down"!

Story in a Paper Bag

This game does require some preparation and thought, but the children (the 8 to 10-year-old group) certainly enjoy it, and it is among the *quiet* games! If twelve children are coming to the party, prepare three paper bags. Into each bag place five or six different objects, round which the children can weave a story. The leader of each group is then presented with a paper bag and told she has five minutes to prepare a story with her team. The group which tells the funniest story, using all the objects, wins and, if there is time, acts the story in front of the others, bringing into play the things in the paper bag. Sometimes the children are given stockings stuffed with objects (in themselves funny), or even pillow-cases, and much quiet and sometimes not-so-quiet amusement ensues as the objects are pulled out one by one.

Word Charades

The 8 to 10-year-olds are quite able to manage "Word Charades". The word chosen is acted in syllables, and the children should be encouraged to make up little scenes with plenty of dialogue. Usually, but not necessarily, the whole word is embodied in a final scene.

Pencil and Paper Games

Children enjoy the novelty of being handed paper and pencil, and being told that now they must put on their thinking caps. A little forethought will ensure that there are some small prizes ready to be handed out at the end of each game, and the winners should be announced with due solemnity and ceremony. Pencil and paper games are invaluable if the party is taking place in a flat where floor space is very limited, but it should always be borne in mind that children are not capable of staying in one place for more than about twenty minutes at a time. These games should, therefore, be spaced out during the afternoon.

A very good game to start off with is "PELMANISM." Obviously, the age of the little guests will guide the organiser in his choice of subjects and the number, but if the children are able to write they will be able to remember a fairly large number of articles.

The children sit in a ring, either on the floor or on chairs. A large tray covered by a cloth or newspaper is then placed in the centre of the ring, so that all the children can see it. The children are then told that underneath the covering is a number of objects, which they will see presently, and that they will be given four minutes to gaze upon them. Each child is then handed a strip of paper and a pencil, and told that the tray will be removed at the end of the four minutes when she must write down as many of the things as she can remember.

Sometimes a number of items from "Mother's Kitchen" are placed on the tray; or "Small Toys from Jimmy's Toy Cupboard", or "Things Found in the Garden". There is an endless choice, and if the game proves popular, as it will among the 8 to 10 group, several different kinds of tray may be produced at intervals. If the children are still writing rather slowly, quite a long time should be given them to prepare their lists. On all such occasions a small bell to signal the "Start" and "Finish", *i.e.*, "Pencils down", is invaluable.

Farmyard Frolic

This is an amusing but noisy game for the small party (up to ten children). When they are all sitting quietly round the room, go up and whisper to each of them the name of an animal. At the word "Go", each child then makes the noise of the animal he has been given. When you can no longer endure the noise, ring the bell and shout "All quiet". Then the children must write down as many of the animal noises as they remember. The one with the most right wins.

Sometimes the players are asked to draw the animals instead of writing down the names, and afterwards given the chance of showing off their art work.

Guess What

A very little preparation is required to produce this game, and the trouble involved is well worth the children's pleasure in it.

Arrange on a small card table in the middle of the room a collection of oddities, *i.e.*, a jam jar with a number of small sweets in it, a pin cushion with some pins, a box of buttons, a bundle of pencils, a jar filled with beans. These should be lettered. The children are then told to write down on their slips of paper the letters A, B, C, D, corresponding to the letters on the oddities. They must then walk round the table, and after a brief glance at the items, must write down against each letter the number they imagine each oddity contains. The game can be played by very small children because only a knowledge of the alphabet and numbers is required. The prize is awarded to the child with the most correct list, *i.e.*, one mark is given in each case to the player whose guess is most nearly correct, and then the marks are added up.

Missing Half

All that is required for this game is a bundle of old picture postcards, or last year's Christmas cards. Cut each card in half, and shoo the children out of the room while you hide the halves. As they return, present each child with the other half, telling him he must find the rest of the card which is hidden somewhere in the room. The children enjoy lifting cushions and looking under carpets. If funds can run to it, two or even three small prizes should be offered, *i.e.* first, second and third.

Missing Letters

Prepare a number of slips of paper, one for each child. On each slip print ten or twelve words with some of the letters missing, *i.e.*, T – G E R. If the children are 9 or 10, the words can be quite difficult. At the word "Go", each child tries to complete the word and finish the list. The first to finish must put her hand up, at the same time shouting: "Me first!"

Pig's Tail

A game which gives a good deal of amusement to the older children. A large tail-less pig is drawn on a very big sheet of brown paper and fixed on the wall. The competitors are then blindfolded, and in turn approach the pig with a coloured chalk to draw in the tail. The one who gets the tail in approximately the right place wins.

Sweet Tooth

For obvious reasons this is a most popular game with every age-group, and is ideal for the small party. Arrange on saucers or dishes six little piles of sweet-tasting things; *i.e.*, a liquorice allsort, a chocolate, a toffee, a raisin, a fig or date, a walnut, etc. Each dish contains exactly the same collection. When the ten children are all blindfolded bring in the tray, and place each child in front of a dish. After consuming the pile of "good-things" the children must then write down what they *think* they have eaten, and the one with the most nearly correct list wins. If the children are very small, make certain that the "good-things" are not too sickly.

The Pig Never Gets His Tail in the Right Place

Treasure Hunts

Hidden Treasure

Treasure Hunts are ideal if there is a fairly large garden and ample protection for the flowers and shrubs against marauding feet and fingers! An Easter Party is just the time for organising an Egg Hunt, chocolate or otherwise. To ensure the more or less even distribution of the eggs, the wisest plan is to wrap a number in different coloured crêpe paper. Each child is then told his colour. If he finds "treasure" which is, say, wrapped in red paper, and his colour is "blue", he must in honour bound replace the "treasure" as he found it, go on his way, and say nothing.

Treasure Hunts are the most exciting things in the world to small children, but they *do* need organising. Obviously one doesn't hide a "treasure" near a rose bed, or beside a lettuce frame! That would be asking for trouble! A few "treasures" placed in very prominent positions will encourage the very small children to persevere in their search. When the party is a mixed age-group one, *i.e.*, running from 4 to 10, it will be easily realised that by giving each child a definite colour to hunt for, the problem of how to prevent the older children snatching all the "treasure" is thereby solved.

It has been known to happen that during an Easter Egg Hunt one small fellow, throwing scruples to the wind, devoured as many eggs as he found, on the spot, irrespective of colour or size. A considerable part of the "treasure" had thus been demolished before he was finally discovered— and banished!

Treasure Hunts for older children are made much more exciting if a trail of clues is laid beforehand, and there is, of course, only one "treasure", which the finder expects to keep!

There's Nothing so Exciting as a Treasure Hunt

The Concert

Strictly speaking this does not come under the heading of "Games", but, on the other hand, no children's party is a party at all if its small guests have not been given the opportunity of saying their "party-pieces". The most successful way of putting this across is to arrange the room as if it were the pit stalls of the theatre. Children catch on to the idea very quickly, and are correspondingly intrigued. Choose the announcer, indicate the stage, and give detailed instructions to the audience on the subject of clapping, etc. It may not be practicable but, if it is, the main light should be switched off and only the standard lamp or table lamp used. This all adds to the realism! Half-way through is, of course, an excellent time to serve out "Ices! Chocolate! Lemonade!" etc., and if you can manage to look like a theatre or cinema Nippy—so much the better!

It is better to have a word with the would-be performers before starting the Concert, so that you can arrange the items with the maximum of variation. Lively gramophone records will add to the "feel" of entertainment, and if there is only a small amount of talent (and that would be surprising, for every child is quite certain she can recite or dance!)

this is the time for the conjurer (it may be only the man-next-door) or somebody who knows how to amuse children.

A very simple and effective way is by "Shadowgraphy", and this may be turned into a Guessing Game quite easily. If the room is small a candle will supply quite sufficient lighting power, and the hands should be held about two feet away from it, and about four feet away from the screen, which should be tightly stretched on a wooden frame. Practice, of course, makes perfect! Most amusing figures can be made to appear on the screen which the children will hugely enjoy, but it is worth the trouble to put in some evenings of practice before the actual Party Day. The very small children will get a thrill out of recognising the different shapes. For scenery—use cardboard cut-outs.

Odder and Odder—Two Hands Make Two Ducks!

77

Games for the Garden
Ball Games

Animal, Vegetable or Mineral

This is a game for the intelligent 8 to 10 age-group. One of the players throws a ball to her friend, and at the same time calls out either "Animal," "Vegetable" or "Mineral". The others all count from one to ten rather quickly. If the child who is touched by the ball does not name something belonging to the kingdom called before the number ten is reached, she is out of the game, and must pay a forfeit at the end of it or, better still, on the spot.

The game can be played indoors. The children sit in a circle, and the one in the middle after turning round two or three times points a stick at her victim and says, "Animal". Adults enjoy this game as much as the intelligent 10-year-olds, and if the party includes a proportion of grown-ups it is useful to include it on the programme.

Catch Who Can

A game for older children. One child stands in the middle of the circle. He is the gardener. Each child in the ring takes the name of a flower or a tree. The gardener, who has been provided with a large soft ball or a balloon, throws it up in the air and calls out a flower name, whose owner must catch the ball before it drops on the ground. If he fails, he falls out of the game, if he succeeds he becomes the gardener.

Dodge Ball

The first condition for playing this game is to ensure that a *soft* ball is used. Baby's woolly ball would be best. The children are scattered on the lawn; one child is given the ball. The ball-holder must then throw the ball at any of the players. He scores a "hit" if the ball touches a player's legs, *below the knee*. Do stress this rule when you are talking about the game so that there is less likelihood of an accident. When he hits anyone the thrower calls "Dead Man" and claims him. "Dead Man" must then assist the thrower by picking up the ball whenever possible and throwing it to him. This continues until all the children are "Dead Men". There are many variations of "Dodge Ball" all equally enjoyable in the eyes of small boys.

Donkey

The children form a large ring in the garden fairly well spaced out. Somebody starts off by throwing the ball to his man on the left. Whenever a player "muffs" his catch, he takes to himself one letter of the word DONKEY. A poor catcher will find himself collecting the letters very quickly to the enjoyment of the others. As soon as he has earned all six letters he is a donkey, and drops out of the game.

If a shortened version of this game is desired, take the word ASS instead of donkey.

French Cricket

For this game a bat and a ball are all the props required. One boy is given the bat and told he must protect his legs with it from the ball. He must not move once he has chosen his position. The other children then take it in turns to aim a ball at his legs. The first child to hit his legs (it is a wise precaution to say "You must not hit him above the knee") becomes batsman.

Please Yourself

The idea is to provide a number of fairly active games all round the garden. The children in pairs wander round, and whichever game attracts them, they start playing. A pile of skipping ropes; a bag of marbles; bat and ball; and "Aunt Sally"; and for the babies perhaps some mechanical toys which belong to the young host. Each little group plays in its corner until the words "All change!" from the grown-up.

NOTE ON AUNT SALLY GAMES

All "Aunt Sally" games are fun, and if the party is a summer one and being held in the garden, this type of game is excellent. A coconut fixed on a firm stand gives a realistic touch to the proceedings, but any kind of object which the players might reasonably be expected to hit is suitable. Here a word of caution is advisable. When playing any kind of "ball" game with little children, make certain the "ball" is fairly soft. Children sometimes lose all sense of direction when they get excited and many a tragedy has occurred at a garden party because a boy has been accidentally struck by a hard ball and perhaps had his eye damaged.

Ping-pong balls aimed at a tilted pail makes an enjoyable game for all ages. To prevent the ping-pong balls bouncing out again in disheartening numbers, line the pail with straw or even newspaper.

Counting-out Rhymes

A book on games would not be complete if something was not said about "Counting-out Rhymes." When there is no obvious reason for choosing a leader, these are invaluable because they avoid any feeling of favouritism. Here are a few of the better known ones.

> *Zeendi, teendi, taehheri, mundheri, bacombe,*
> *Hecturi, zecturi, aover, daover-dek.*

This is quite a tongue twister, but the children enjoy it immensely. The quicker the words are said the more telling the effect. Its origin incidentally goes back thousands of years to a form of counting used by the shepherds of Strathclyde.

One with a familiar sound is:

> *Eetle ottle*
> *Black bottle*
> *Eetle ottle*
> *Out!*

"I Hope I'm Not Last Man In!"

And another one widely accepted by children is:

> *Eeny, meeny, miny, mo*
> *Catch a nigger by his toe.*
> *When he squeals let him go.*
> *Eeny, meeny, miny, mo*
> *O–U–T spells out.*

A tongue twister which will make the children laugh is:

Counting-out Rhymes

Eeri, orie, ickery, am
Pick ma nick and stick ma slam
Oram, scoram, pick ma noram,
Shee, show, sham, shutter
You—are—out.

This is not such a well-known rhyme, but the children will be glad to learn it:

Elder, belder, limber, lock
Three wives in a clock
Sit and sing, and call a spring
O—U—T spells out!

Another favourite with children down the ages is:

As I went up Hicky-picky hill,
I met two frichty-picky children.
They asked me this, and they
  asked me that
And they asked me the colour of
  my best Sunday hat
(Green) G—R—E—E—N spells green
And O—U—T spells out!

And here is one to encourage their counting:

One, two, three, four, five,
Yes, I caught a fish alive
Six, seven, eight, nine, ten,
But I let it go again.

Counting-out Rhymes

Why did you let it go?
Because it bit my finger so!
Which finger did it bite?
The little one here on the right!

The fact that this Counting-out Rhyme takes rather longer to enact gives rise to a pleasurable feeling of excitement as the Counter-out goes up and down the line gently touching each child as she pronounces each word.

A general favourite because it is so easy to remember is:

One potato,
Two potato
Three potato—Four
Five potato,
Six potato,
Seven potato—More.

The children hold out their hands, palms outwards, and the Counter-out brings her own hand down on their palms as she passes along the line. As she reaches the word "More" the child she is facing drops one of her hands, and the Rhyme is chanted until finally one of the players has dropped both hands.

The hostess who is in charge of organising the games might spend a few useful moments memorising some of these Counting-out Rhymes. Not only will she surprise the children by talking their language, but she will delight and entertain them by the variety she produces for each succeeding game.

Programmes

As suggested in the Introduction, a "Programme of Events" not only gives the organiser a sense of security, but is a most useful last line of defence when differences of opinion arise as to what is to follow next.

Here then are two specimen Programmes. These are by no means the last word on Programmes, for age, physical stamina, space and funds are all factors to be considered when compiling Programmes. A small room in a small flat will not lend itself to romping games, and these should never even be hinted at! Again, where there is a garden, the Programme might usefully include a number of Outdoor Games, weather permitting.

It is important to be very definite about the time the Party begins, and the time it ends. Nothing is more trying than to have parents "dribbling in" a good twenty minutes after the hour at which you hopefully imagined the Party would be over.

The first Programme is for a Party held indoors, and scheduled to run approximately three hours. From experience the most convenient time for such a Party to commence is half-past three in the afternoon. This allows the tiny tots to have had their afternoon rest before setting out.

THE PROGRAMME

Mary's Jane's Party

Guests arrive

Tea

Crackers

Games

Spinning the Platter
The Farmer Wants a Wife
I Wrote a Letter
Johnny Rover

Balloons

Games with Balloons

INTERVAL

Ices — drinks — sweets

CONCERT

Pencil and Paper Games

Guess What
Farmyard Frolic

Games with Movement

London Bridge is Broken Down
Lubin Loo
Musical Chairs
Musical Statues

Distribution of Prizes

Arrival of Parents   Farewells

Programmes

This a Programme for Peter's Party. His birthday falls in June, and, weather permitting, it is proposed to hold the party entirely out-of-doors. The Programme is printed in coloured chalk on strong brown paper and pinned on to a tree. Two wooden forms are placed in a shady part of the garden; cabbage leaves serve as plates, and these rest on well-scrubbed bare wooden tables. With a little ingenuity, the table can be effectively decorated with garden produce, and the children love the improvisations.

THE PROGRAMME

Guests arrive

Tea

TREASURE HUNT

Hark the Robbers

Oranges and Lemons

Down in the Jungle

Jumping the River

A short "rest" period. Children lie flat on the grass (providing it is dry) or on mats, and shut their eyes.

Ices — drinks — sweets

Train Tag

Mary's Sunbonnet

Jumble Sale

CONCERT or COMMUNITY SINGING

Distribution of Prizes

General "clean-up"   Arrival of Parents   Farewells

Road to Success

From the moment the invitation cards go out, the children start looking forward to the party. On the great day itself they are keyed up to a note of expectancy. Wise planning and forethought will turn the simplest party into an event which fulfils their expectations.

If a large number of children are expected, try to give each one a special place for his or her coat and slipper bag. So often much of the end-of-party happiness is rubbed off, when the coats and hats and gloves are lost or mislaid.

A pleasant way of overcoming any shyness and strangeness on the part of the newly arrived little guests is to present them with little cards on which are printed fairy tale or pantomime characters. When they have shed their cloaks and shawls, pin a card on each of them. "You are Red Riding Hood. Now go and find Mr. Wolf." The children quickly forget their shyness in the excitement of looking for their partner.

If the party is by way of being something rather special, one idea which lifts it out of the ordinary run of parties is to decorate the room and table with some definite scene in mind. "The Magic Wood", or "The Smuggler's Cave", or

"The Pirates' Cabin". Surprisingly little trouble is involved to get an effect, and the children's imaginations supply most of the detail.

Table decorations might further the illusion. It is much better to start with tea almost at once. For one thing the children are sure to be wondering what there is to eat! And for another, in a small house or flat, very often only one room is available. It is far more satisfactory, therefore, to use the time before the guests arrive in preparing the tea table. When tea is over, the table can be cleared quickly, and the decks made ready for action.

Crackers are almost as essential as balloons, but a box of tiny ones will give as much fun as the large ones, and are much less expensive to buy. A sound rule is to say "No" very firmly to any cracker-pulling until after the cups and glasses are removed from the table.

Generally speaking, rich iced cakes are never a success. Children like plain meringues, chocolate biscuits, sugared buns, jellies and ice cream. Plates of thinly cut buttered bread are more easily prepared than sandwiches and just as much appreciated. Dishes of sliced peeled apple lightly sprinkled with sugar, and now that bananas are more plentiful, plain biscuits with slices of banana on top, will appeal to children of all ages, and are not too sickly.

But the scope of this book as we noted in the Introduction, wide as it is, is not meant to include eatables; it has been impossible, however, to omit just these few odd remarks about what children like and dislike, for after all the success of the party may stand or fall on what there is to eat. Satisfied, happy children will play the games with just all that more enthusiasm which makes the party "A jolly good show", or just "It wasn't bad".

Although many of the games described in this book can be played and enjoyed as much by the 5s as the 10s, the problem of how best to run a party of mixed age-groups still remains. It can be a very real one, for few parents nowadays can face up to two parties in the same year, and yet if Jim is 5 and Penny 9, what to do?

A headmistress faced an almost similar problem in this way. Her small but rather exclusive boarding school was in danger of being "split" into two camps. There was no liaison between her senior girls and her very young juniors. She solved the problem by making the senior girls at the top of the school into "mothers". Each mother was given a number of "children" and the family group did everything together in recreational periods. As a result the whole spirit of the school improved enormously.

If this plan is adopted at the outset of the party, the more senior guests will adore being "mothers" and "fathers". They will want to play games which delight their "babies", and there will be none of that feeling of superiority which can spoil any gathering of children. Take the seniors into your confidence, give them a feeling of responsibility, tell them that you count on them to make the party successful, and you will be surprised how well they react and what a help they can be when it comes to amusing the little ones.

A sound idea is to have two sets of prizes for all the games—one for the under 6s and one for the overs. If you do this, the little ones will not smart under any sense of injustice if the big ones always seem to be winning.

But games and competitions for the older children should never be altogether overlooked. Be fair! When the older children are playing a game which the babies would only spoil, arrange to have some quiet sitting games for the infants, and keep them as much in the corners as possible. If they want to watch, make them sit down well out of the range of activity. Then everybody will be happy.

And one word more! Games are games! Some children are bad losers! Make it quite clear that you think very highly of a "good" loser. A word of praise at the beginning to the child who loses a game and who still smiles will set the whole tone of the party. Deal with the "whiners" tactfully but firmly; they will be grateful to you by the end of the afternoon.

Parties are fun! Fun for the children—a nightmare to the grown-ups! But they needn't be! And this time, let us hope, the party will be fun for you too!

Index